Fourteen
Festive So.....

ex libris

Candlestick Press

Published by:
Candlestick Press,
Diversity House, 72 Nottingham Road, Arnold, Nottingham UK NG5 6LF
www.candlestickpress.co.uk

Design and typesetting by Diversity Creative Marketing Solutions Ltd.,
www.diversity.agency

Printed by Ratcliff & Roper Print Group, Nottinghamshire, UK

Selection and Introduction © James Nash, 2017

Cover illustration © Woman from Baku/Shutterstock

Candlestick Press monogram © Barbara Shaw, 2008

© Candlestick Press, 2017

Donation to Samaritans www.samaritans.org

ISBN 978 1 907598 59 3

Acknowledgements:

The poems in this pamphlet are reprinted from the following books, all by
permission of the publishers listed unless stated otherwise. Every effort has been
made to trace the copyright holders of the poems published in this book. The editor
and publisher apologise if any material has been included without permission or
without the appropriate acknowledgement, and would be glad to be told of anyone
who has not been consulted. Thanks are due to all the copyright holders cited below
for their kind permission:

Joolz Denby, poem as yet unpublished, by kind permission of the author.

Erik Didriksen, *Pop Sonnets on Tumblr* (Quirk Books, 2015) by permission of
Rogers, Coleridge and White Literary Agency.

Kevin Holloway, poem as yet unpublished, by kind permission of the author.

Aileen Lucia Fisher, *Skip Around the Year* (New York: Thomas Y. Crowell, 1967).
Copyright © 1967, 1985 by Aileen Fisher. Reprinted with the permission of Marian
Reiner Literary Agency.

Claude McKay, *Complete Poems* (Chicago University of Illinois Press, 2004) 'To
Winter' © 1920 is used with the permission of the Literary Estate for the works of
Claude McKay.

James Nash, poem as yet unpublished, by kind permission of the author.

May Sarton, *Collected Poems* (W. W. Norton, 1993) by permission of the publisher
and A. M. Heath and Co. Ltd.

Anne Stevenson, *Poems 1960-2000* (Bloodaxe Books, 2000)
www.bloodaxebooks.com.

David Tait, *Love's Loose Ends* (smith|doorstop, 2011) by permission of the
publisher.

Judith Wright, *Collected Poems* (HarperCollins Australia, 2016) by permission of
the Estate of Judith Wright.

All permissions cleared courtesy of Swift Permissions (swiftpermissions@
gmail.com). Where poets are no longer living, their dates are given.

Contents

Introduction

How much information, thought and feeling is packed into
the traditional fourteen line sonnet (I've let two into this little
collection with fifteen lines and even one with thirteen lines)
and again how many memories and reflections are part of that
mid-winter season when we look to light as a symbol of hope?
Put the form and the season together and you have a potent
human mix of celebration and of nostalgia and loss.

It was such a pleasure to rediscover 'Sonnet in the Snow' by
David Tait, because it was his sonnet-writing workshop at Leeds
University, when he was still a student, which set me on my own
sonnet-writing path. There are poems here by Judith Wright and
Anne Stevenson, major poets of the last hundred years, whilst
John Clare still sings from a much earlier time.

It would be odd to have such a collection, however short, which
did not contain a sonnet by Shakespeare because it was he who
gave us a form with its iambic pentameter and rhyming scheme
that still works today for many modern poets.

And then there were the discoveries; the minor poets who wrote
major poems, the great poets who used this miniature form to
illuminate the season. It is the writer's job to celebrate all of
this but also to recognise and explore the other side of things,
the loneliness, the loss and the meditations on deeper themes,
so we have joyfulness leavened with more muted emotions, and,
because these are sonnets, many of them are also poems of love.

There are Christian, Jewish and pagan pieces here. There is
one outrageous pop-song parody which made me laugh. I hope
you relish the real and metaphorical festive seasons to be found
within them, from melting snow to angels and, ultimately, to joy.

James Nash

Sonnet in the Snow

I knew it would stick, so I woke up early
to put on my coat, and wrote you
a sonnet in the snow. I staked the first claim
of your street's snowflake footprints, then sketched it

on the rooftops of four cars – the chalk crunch
as I traced words on metal – looping letters
that curled precise for your eyes. When you opened
the blinds it would melt your cold heart.

Though of course it didn't work out like this.
The woman next door drove off with stanza two.
And I watched by the hedge as the blizzard summoned day,
and school kids took the couplet for a man made of snow.

Your sonnet in the snow glowed pale below the moon,
though your curtains never opened. It had gone by noon.

David Tait

To Winter

Stay, season of calm love and soulful snows!
There is a subtle sweetness in the sun,
The ripples on the stream's breast gaily run,
The wind more boisterously by me blows,
And each succeeding day now longer grows.
The birds a gladder music have begun,
The squirrel, full of mischief and of fun,
From maples' topmost branch the brown twig throws.
I read these pregnant signs, know what they mean:
I know that thou art making ready to go.
Oh stay! I fled a land where fields are green
Always, and palms wave gently to and fro,
And winds are balmy, blue brooks ever sheen,
To ease my heart of its impassioned woe.

Claude McKay (1890 – 1948)

This House

which represents you, as my bones do, waits,
all pores open, for the stun of snow. Which will come
as it always comes, between breaths, between nights
of no wind and days of the nulled sun.
And has to be welcome. All instinct wants to anticipate
faceless fields, a white road drawn
through dependent firs, the soldered glare of lakes.

Is it wanting you here to want the winter in?
I breathe you back into your square house and begin
to live here roundly. This year will be between,
not in, four seasons. Do you hear already the wet
rumble of thaw? Stones. Sky. Streams.
Sun. Those might be swallows at the edge of sight
returning to last year's nest in the crook of the porchlight.

Anne Stevenson

Winter

The small wind whispers through the leafless hedge
Most sharp and chill, where the light snowy flakes
Rest on each twig and spike of wither'd sedge,
Resembling scatter'd feathers;—vainly breaks
The pale split sunbeam through the frowning cloud,
On Winter's frowns below—from day to day
Unmelted still he spreads his hoary shroud,
In dithering pride on the pale traveller's way,
Who, croodling, hastens from the storm behind
Fast gathering deep and black, again to find
His cottage-fire and corner's sheltering bounds;
Where, haply, such uncomfortable days
Make musical the wood-sap's frizzling sounds,
And hoarse loud bellows puffing up the blaze.

John Clare (1793 – 1864)

Light the Festive Candles
(For Hanukkah)

Light the first of eight tonight –
the farthest candle to the right.

Light the first and second, too,
when tomorrow's day is through.

Then light three, and then light four –
every dusk one candle more

Till all eight burn bright and high,
honoring a day gone by

When the Temple was restored,
rescued from the Syrian lord,

And an eight-day feast proclaimed –
The Festival of Lights – well named

To celebrate the joyous day
when we regained the right to pray
to our one God in our own way.

Aileen Lucia Fisher (1906 – 2002)

Christmas Light

When everyone had gone
I sat in the library
With the small silent tree,
She and I alone.
How softly she shone!

And for the first time then
For the first time this year,
I felt reborn again,
I knew love's presence near.

Love distant, love detached
And strangely without weight,
Was with me in the night
When everyone had gone
And the garland of pure light
Stayed on, stayed on.

May Sarton (1912 – 1995)

Free

The herd of mares broke their hobbles
And bolted through the open field gate
Of the common ground, frayed manes
Whipping the cold and their colts stilting
Leggy on the ice iron turf, the steam of
Their racing blood as they wheeled onto
The main road a frost spume, and the
White bolus of the wild winter moon
Shone in their round, black, rolling eyes
As they wove through the braking slew of
Cars and ran for freedom and the distant moorland;
City horses shaggy as Christmas tinsel
Crazy with the thin, cold air and hope.

Joolz Denby

Saint Nicholas

Employed through the super-store's seniors scheme
and 'Greeter of the Month' four times in a row,
Tony had seemed the member of the team
most suited to the task. He was troubled though.
Not by the costume and false white beard,
but by the bare faced lies he'd have to tell.
The manager cajoled, gently steered:
' ... enriching Christmas ... you'll do it all so well'.

Tony paused, then reluctantly agreed.
He ho-hoed through weeks of, 'Now, what have you
asked Santa for?' Until, on Christmas Day, freed
from disguise and lies, he woke, went down to
his comfy chair. There, a gift: 'From Nicholas, His Grace'.
And sooty footprints, from and to the fireplace.

Kevin Holloway

Sonnet 73

That time of year thou mayst in me behold
When yellow leaves, or none, or few, do hang
Upon those boughs which shake against the cold,
Bare ruin'd choirs, where late the sweet birds sang.
In me thou seest the twilight of such day
As after sunset fadeth in the west,
Which by and by black night doth take away,
Death's second self, that seals up all in rest.
In me thou seest the glowing of such fire
That on the ashes of his youth doth lie,
As the death-bed whereon it must expire,
Consum'd with that which it was nourish'd by.
 This thou perceiv'st, which makes thy love more strong,
 To love that well which thou must leave ere long.

William Shakespeare (1564 – 1616)

To One Poem in a Silent Time

Who looked for thee, thou little song of mine?
  This winter of a silent poet's heart
  Is suddenly sweet with thee. But what thou art,
Mid-winter flower, I would I could divine.
Art thou a last one, orphan of thy line?
  Did the dead summer's last warmth foster thee?
  Or is Spring folded up unguessed in me,
And stirring out of sight,—and thou the sign?

Where shall I look—backwards or to the morrow
  For others of thy fragrance, secret child?
    Who knows if last things or if first things claim
    thee?
—Whether thou be the last smile of my sorrow,
  Or else a joy too sweet, a joy too wild.
    How, my December violet, shall I name thee?

Alice Meynell (1847 – 1922)

Sonnet for Christmas

I saw our golden years on a black gale,
our time of love spilt in the furious dust.
"O we are winter-caught, and we must fail,"
said the dark dream, "and time is overcast."
—And woke into the night; but you were there,
and small as seed in the wild dark we lay.
Small as seed under the gulfs of air
is set the stubborn heart that waits for day.
I saw our love the root that holds the vine
in the enduring earth, that can reply,
"Nothing shall die unless for me it die.
Murder and hate and love alike are mine";
and therefore fear no winter and no storm
while in the knot of earth that root lies warm.

Judith Wright (1915 – 2000)

I have no list detailing my desires
for presents to receive this winter night,
for nothing old Saint Nich'las might acquire
could bring my aching heart sincere delight.
The gift I want shall not come wrapp'd in bows,
so I shall presents 'neath the tree neglect;
I will not even hope for downy snows
to leave the world in brilliant white bedeck'd.
Instead, I'll bow my head and pray that Fate
shall steer thee to my doorway, where I stand
beneath a sprig of mistletoe and wait
for thee to come and follow its command.
  – O let my Yuletide wishes granted be;
  yea, all I want this Christmas night is thee.

Mariah Carey, 'All I Want for Christmas Is You!'

Erik Didriksen

Shepherd's Sonnet

It seems with each Christmas that comes around
God has some changes for my body planned,
And everything I do comes with a sound,
A sighing when I sit, exhaling when I stand.
My joints creak now on winter nights,
When memories stir in my heart once more;
We came from the hills to a sky of lights
And I knelt on the snow in reverent awe.
So baby, lying in the manger there,
It's as if each year you're born anew,
This old man offers these sounds as prayer,
Dedicates each ache and pain to you.
You'll surely not remember who I am,
I was the shepherd boy who brought the lamb.

James Nash

To Joy

Lo, I am happy, for my eyes have seen
Joy glowing here before me, face to face;
His wings were arched above me for a space,
I kissed his lips, no bitter came between.
The air is vibrant where his feet have been,
And full of song and color is his place.
His wondrous presence sheds about a grace
That lifts and hallows all that once was mean.
I may not sorrow for I saw the light,
Tho' I shall walk in valley ways for long,
I still shall hear the echo of the song,—
My life is measured by its one great height.
Joy holds more grace than pain can ever give,
And by my glimpse of joy my soul shall live.

Sara Teasdale (1844 – 1933)